BOSTON COMMON PRESS
Brookline, Massachusetts

2000

Other titles in the *Cook's Illustrated*
How to Cook Series

BOSTON COMMON PRESS
Brookline, Massachusetts

2000

Other titles in the *Cook's Illustrated*
How to Cook Series

HOW TO COOK CHINESE FAVORITES

An illustrated step-by-step guide
to foolproof soups, dumplings,
steamed fish, classic stir-fries,
rice dishes, and noodles.

THE COOK'S ILLUSTRATED LIBRARY

Illustrations by John Burgoyne

Boston Common Press
17 Station Street
Brookline, Massachusetts 02445

ISBN 0-936184-45-0
Library of Congress Cataloging-in-Publication Data
The Editors of *Cook's Illustrated*
How to cook Chinese favorites: An illustrated step-by-step guide to foolproof soups,
dumplings, steamed fish, classic stir-fries, rice dishes, and noodles./The Editors of
Cook's Illustrated
1st ed.

Includes 31 recipes and 16 illustrations
ISBN 0-936184-45-0 (hardback): $14.95
I. Cooking. I. Title
2000

Manufactured in the United States of America

Distributed by Boston Common Press, 17 Station Street, Brookline, MA 02445.

Cover and text design: Amy Klee
Recipe development: Elizabeth Germain
Series editor: Jack Bishop

CONTENTS

introduction

For most Americans, Chinese cooking is something to eat out or order in. Very few of us have actually visited China to see first-hand how dishes are prepared. The distance between the two countries and cultures creates the distinct impression that Chinese food is difficult to prepare at home.

Of course, the more than 1 billion people living in China would argue otherwise, and they would be right. Unfortunately, the culinary ingredients and traditions in China are so different from those in the United States that it makes little sense for the American cook to try to duplicate authentic Chinese cooking at home.

Our goal for this book is much more modest. We wanted to take favorite Chinese restaurant dishes—things like egg drop soup and kung pao chicken—and make them work for the American home cook.

This necessitated a couple of compromises up front. Exotic ingredients, available only to shoppers in Chinatown, were out. While we strongly recommend that you make an effort to visit an Asian grocery store (something found in most cities and suburban areas) to buy fresh noodles, we realize that not everyone can. That's why we tested six substitutes before discovering that fresh linguine can be used in place of Chinese noodles to make lo mein.

Our exhaustive kitchen testing uncovered some other surprises. Peanut butter makes great cold sesame noodles. Oyster sauce is the secret to richly flavored lo mein. Greasing a metal steamer basket keeps wontons from sticking, but fish will stick unless the basket is lined with cabbage.

This book is filled with the kind of information that can be uncovered only by means of repeated testing. Detailed explanations will help you understand why certain techniques work and which ingredients are essential.

How to Cook Chinese Favorites is the 23rd book in the How to Cook series published by *Cook's Illustrated,* a bimonthly publication on American home cooking. Turn to the beginning of the book for a complete list of the titles in the series. To order other books, call us at (800) 611-0759 or visit us online at www.cooksillustrated.com. For a free trial copy of *Cook's,* call (800) 526-8442.

Christopher P. Kimball
Publisher and Editor
Cook's Illustrated

chapter one

BASICS OF CHINESE COOKING

EFORE YOU COOK, IT'S IMPORTANT TO UNDER-
stand the role of several important pieces of
equipment, a handful of basic ingredients, and
some classic Chinese cooking techniques.

EQUIPMENT

WOKS VERSUS SKILLETS

Many Chinese dishes, especially stir-fries, depend on plenty
of heat to caramelize sugars, deepen flavors through intense
browning, and drive off excess liquid. The problem is that
the Chinese wok and the typical American stovetop are a
lousy match, capable of generating only moderate heat.
Woks are conical because in China they traditionally rest in

8

cylindrical pits containing the fire. Flames lick the bottom and sides of the pan so that food cooks remarkably quickly. A wok is not designed for stovetop cooking, where heat comes only from the bottom.

We think a horizontal heat source requires a horizontal pan. For stir-frying at home, we recommend a large skillet, 12 to 14 inches in diameter, with a nonstick coating. Size is important because you want foods to cook in a single layer, which causes them to brown rather than steam. The nonstick coating allows you to use less oil.

In our testing of major brands of nonstick skillets, All-Clad and Calphalon came out on top. Both brands are sturdy but not overly heavy, so you can easily move these pans around the stovetop. They conduct heat well, allowing the surface of the skillet to become very hot, but their handles, which are made from hollowed-out metal, stay cooler than solid metal handles. A handle with a removable plastic sheath is ideal when stir-frying.

▪ SHOVELS

Chinese cooks use shovel-shaped spatulas to move food around in a wok. The same tool works well in a skillet. To protect nonstick surfaces, use plastic or wooden implements, not metal. We prefer large shovels with a wide, thin blade and long, heat-resistant handle.

▉ STEAMERS

Chinese cooks often prepare foods in bamboo steamers. We have provided instructions for using a bamboo steamer in recipes throughout this book, but all recipes have also been tested on a collapsible metal steamer basket, an item American home cooks are more likely to own. Make sure to buy a large steamer basket, at least 11 inches in diameter. Smaller steamers won't be able to hold four pieces of fish or a full batch of dumplings.

INGREDIENTS

▉ ASIAN SESAME OIL

Also known as dark or toasted sesame oil, this aromatic, medium-brown oil is used as a seasoning in Chinese cooking. Because its smoke point is quite low (the oil burns at fairly low temperatures), it is not advisable to cook with sesame oil. Use some in a sauce, or toss noodles with a little sesame oil for a flavor boost. Don't confuse this product with regular sesame oil, which is pressed from untoasted seeds and has a medium yellow color. Store an open bottle in the refrigerator to prolong freshness.

▉ CANNED CHICKEN BROTH

For most soups, we recommend homemade stock. For Chinese sauces, where just a few tablespoons of chicken broth are needed, store-bought versions are fine. Because canned broth is reduced in so many sauces, we recommend the use of low-sodium products to prevent sauces from becoming overly salty. Canned broths from Swanson's and Campbell's (which are owned by the same company) have consistently received top ratings in our taste tests. We find broths sold in aseptic cartons to be more flavorful than canned broths, which undergo a longer sterilization process.

CHILI PASTE

This thick, bright red seasoning looks like ketchup but is made from crushed chile peppers, vinegar, and, usually, garlic. Brands vary from mild to incendiary, so taste before using. Store opened bottles in the refrigerator.

FERMENTED BLACK BEANS

Chinese fermented black beans have a salty, beany flavor that adds an intriguing savory note to many dishes, especially those made with seafood. Nothing more than salted black beans, this product is sold in bags in Asian food stores and keeps indefinitely in the freezer. Make sure to buy beans that are soft to the touch, not hard or shriveled. Some sources suggest rinsing fermented black beans before using them, but we find this unnecessary as long as you have purchased quality beans that are not overly salty.

▪▪ OYSTER SAUCE

This thick, dark brown sauce is made from fermented oysters, salt, and spices. It lends a meaty, savory note to foods as well as a rich, dark color. We find that it is an essential ingredient when making lo mein and some stir-fry sauces. Some supermarkets may stock this item. Otherwise, an Asian grocery is your best bet. We have used Lee Kum Kee Premium Oyster-Flavored Sauce with excellent results. Don't let the words "oyster-flavored" throw you. Read labels and make sure the sauce contains oysters rather than MSG (monosodium glutamate). Refrigerate bottles once opened.

▪▪ RICE VINEGAR

Several kinds of vinegar are made from rice in various parts of Asia. The most common type is clear and very mild—even a bit sweet. Rice vinegar has far less acidity than most Western vinegars (4 percent versus 6 to 7 percent in most wine vinegars), so it is hard to use other vinegars in its place. Luckily, most supermarkets carry this staple.

▪▪ RICE WINE

Rice wine is an Asian equivalent for dry sherry. It is used in sauces and marinades to add complexity to the flavor of a dish. Dry sherry can be substituted for rice wine, although it tends to taste more harsh and less complex.

■■ SOY SAUCE

Few condiments are as misunderstood as soy sauce, the pungent, fragrant, fermented flavoring that's a mainstay in Asian cooking. Its simple, straightforward composition—equal parts soybeans and a roasted grain, usually wheat, plus water and salt—belies the subtle, sophisticated contribution it makes as an all-purpose seasoning, flavor enhancer, tabletop condiment, and dipping sauce. The three products consumers are likely to encounter are regular soy sauce, light soy sauce (made with a higher percentage of water and hence lower in sodium), and tamari (made with fermented soybeans, water, and salt—no wheat). Tamari generally has a stronger flavor and thicker consistency than soy sauce. It is traditionally used in Japanese cooking, not Chinese.

In a tasting of leading soy sauces, we found that products aged according to ancient customs are superior to synthetic sauces, such as La Choy's, which are made in a day and almost always contain hydrolyzed vegetable protein. Our favorite soy sauce, Eden Selected Shoyu Soy Sauce (*shoyu* is the Japanese word for soy sauce), is aged for three years.

TECHNIQUES

■■ STIR-FRYING

In developing recipes for our book *How to Stir-Fry*, we tested all the important variables in this unique cooking process. For this book, we decided to develop two classic stir-fries—kung pao chicken and beef and broccoli in garlic sauce. Because the recipes for these stir-fries are based on techniques we developed for *How to Stir-Fry*, it is useful to repeat some of the key findings here.

The most important thing to remember when stir-frying is to use enough heat. Stir-frying must happen quickly. Foods need to brown, not steam, and a superhot pan is essential. As noted on page 9, we think a nonstick skillet is the best vessel for stir-frying on a conventional stovetop.

A stir-fry consists of four major components: protein, vegetables, aromatics (garlic, ginger, and scallions), and sauce.

We found that a simple marinade of soy sauce and sherry (or rice wine) really boosts the flavor of the protein. The protein should be stir-fried first, then removed from the pan so other ingredients can be cooked.

Vegetables should be cut fairly small. We found it best to add them to the pan in batches to keep the pan from cooling down too much. We think a good stir-fry is two parts vegetables and one part protein. For four people, this means 1½ pounds vegetables to ¾ pound of meat, poultry, or seafood.

Stir-fries must contain the three basic Chinese seasonings of garlic, ginger, and scallions. We found that these aromatics tend to burn if added to the pan too early. To keep this from happening, we clear a space in the center of the pan once the vegetables have been cooked, add the aromatics and a little oil, and then stir-fry them just until fragrant. At this point, the cooked protein is returned to the pan, along with the sauce, which prevents the aromatics from scorching.

Stir-fry sauces must be bold. We found that cornstarch-thickened sauces are often thick and gloppy. In our tests, sauces made without cornstarch were cleaner-tasting and are preferred.

◖ SLICING MEAT

Thinly sliced meat is a hallmark of Chinese cooking, whether it's thin strips of pork in lo mein or pieces of flank steak in a stir-fry. Thick slabs of meat will be flabby and may not marry well with other ingredients, so make sure to use a sharp knife when slicing chicken, pork, and beef. We find that partially freezing meat (an hour is more than enough time) firms up its texture and makes slicing easier.

◖ READYING *MISE EN PLACE*

Mise en place is a French term, but it applies to Chinese cooking as well. Simply stated, it means having all ingredients prepared and close at hand before you start cooking.

chapter two

SOUPS

THE CHAPTER COVERS THREE CLASSIC Chinese soups: wonton, egg drop, and hot and sour. Each begins with chicken stock. Given the relative importance of the stock in wonton and egg drop soups, homemade stock is preferable in these recipes. It is less important in hot-and-sour soup, which contains many strongly flavored ingredients.

WONTON SOUP

In many respects, wonton soup is the simplest Chinese soup to prepare—that is, if you have dumplings and stock on hand. In our testing we focused on the dumplings and other ingredients that are sometimes added to the broth.

The traditional wonton shape is a triangle with the two corners brought together. Some sources favor the traditional shape, while others recommend a tortellini-shaped wonton because leakage of the filling is supposedly less likely. In tortellini, the top corner (the one not bound to the others) is folded down.

We prepared both shapes and had no trouble with leaking in either case, as long as we were careful to brush the edges of the wrappers with water to create a tight seal. The triangular shape was the unanimous favorite for two reasons—tradition and texture. It met people's visual expectations (the tortellini evoked comments about Chinese-Italian food), and, when properly cooked, it allows for a large part of the wrapper to turn silky smooth, just as great noodles do in broth. The tortellini shape was too chewy and condensed in comparison.

The next question was the filling. We tested all of the dumpling fillings created for chapter 3 of this book. All were delicious, but the rich pork filling was deemed the most authentic. For a lighter soup, we suggest using chicken in place of pork (as directed in the filling recipe) or turning to the shrimp filling.

With shape and filling decided, our next concern was cooking the wontons. Boiling the wontons directly in the soup turned them mushy and slimy and had the effect of

17

clouding the stock. Of the other two options, boiling and steaming them separately, we found boiling to produce the best results. The wrappers retained some body and yet remained tender and supple in the mouth. The steamed wontons were chewy.

The final issue to be tested was what ingredients (if any) to add to the broth. This area is fairly subjective, and we decided to stay close to tradition. Greens and scallions were deemed a must. (Napa cabbage, iceberg lettuce, or spinach are all good choices for the greens.) Carrots, while not absolutely necessary, are a common ingredient and add color to the soup.

Wonton Soup

serves 6 to 8

➤ *N O T E : The wontons are cooked separately in boiling water and then added to the broth. Try to time things so that the broth is already simmering when you cook the wontons.*

Wontons

  32   **wonton wrappers**
  ½   **recipe Pork Filling for dumplings (page 41)**
       Salt

Soup Base

  2   **quarts chicken stock**
  ½   **cup shredded greens (napa cabbage, spinach, or iceberg lettuce)**
  3   **medium scallions, finely chopped**
  2   **tablespoons grated carrot from half of small carrot (optional)**
       Salt and ground black pepper

I N S T R U C T I O N S :

1. Fill and seal wontons (see figures 1 through 3, pages 20–21). Place wontons on large baking sheet covered with parchment or wax paper and refrigerate to firm up, at least 20 minutes or up to several hours. (Or place baking sheet in freezer until wontons are frozen, about 3 hours. Transfer to airtight container and freeze up to 1 month.)

2. Bring 4 quarts of water to a boil in large pot. Salt water to taste and add wontons. Cook until wontons are tender, 3 to 4 minutes (add 2 minutes if frozen). Lift wontons from water with slotted spoon and set aside on large plate.

3. Meanwhile, bring stock to a simmer in large soup kettle. Add greens, scallions, and carrots (if using) and simmer to blend flavors, 3 to 4 minutes. Add cooked wontons and simmer until wontons are heated through, 1 to 2 minutes. Season with salt and pepper to taste and serve immediately.

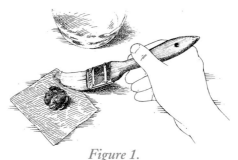

Figure 1.
Place a wonton skin on a flat, dry work surface with a corner pointing toward you. Place 1 teaspoon of filling in the center of the wrapper. Brush the edges lightly with water.

Figure 2.
Fold the wonton in half, away from you, making a triangle.
Press edges firmly to seal.

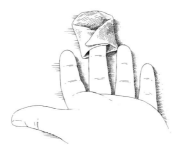

Figure 3.
Lightly brush the 2 corners nearest you with water, fold them
over your finger, and press together to seal.

EGG DROP SOUP

Egg drop soup is basically thickened chicken stock with ribbons of coagulated egg. Ideally, the egg is fully cooked but still tender. There are two schools of thought as to how to accomplish this. In one, the eggs are poured onto the surface of the simmering broth and allowed to set without stirring. The eggs are then broken up with a fork. The other method calls for whisking the eggs into the broth and then allowing them to set without further stirring.

When we laid the eggs on the surface of the soup and allowed them to set up without stirring, the egg remained in large blobs. Once the eggs were set, even vigorous stirring with a fork failed to break them up into small enough pieces.

Whisking in the eggs breaks them into small bits that set up into thinner ribbons. We found it best to add the eggs slowly and then let them cook for another 30 to 60 seconds, undisturbed, to ensure that they are fully set.

Although some sources suggest that the eggs alone will give egg drop soup its characteristic thick texture, we did not find this to be the case. Most recipes added cornstarch to give the soup some viscosity. The texture is important because the ribbons of egg will fall to the bottom of a bowl of thin, brothy soup. We found that two tablespoons of cornstarch (dissolved in two tablespoons of water) thickened two quarts of stock sufficiently to suspend the ribbons of egg.

Egg Drop Soup
serves 6 to 8

➤ **N O T E :** *Timing is essential in this recipe. Because the corn-starch will lose its thickening power if simmered too long, the remaining ingredients must be added quickly once the cornstarch goes into the pot. Egg drop soup will not hold and should be served immediately.*

- **2** quarts chicken stock
- **1** tablespoon soy sauce
  Salt
- **2** tablespoons cornstarch
- **2** medium scallions, chopped fine
- **2** tablespoons minced fresh cilantro leaves
- **4** large eggs, beaten in a measuring cup

■ I N S T R U C T I O N S :

1. Bring stock to a simmer in large saucepan over medium-high heat. Add soy sauce and salt to taste.

2. Combine cornstarch and 2 tablespoons water in small bowl and stir until smooth. Whisk cornstarch mixture into broth until it thickens slightly, about 1 minute. Stir in scal-lions and cilantro.

3. Slowly add eggs to broth (see figure 4, page 24). Let eggs stand in broth without mixing until they are set, less than 1 minute. Once they have set, break up egg ribbons with a fork. Serve immediately.

Figure 4.
Whisk the broth so that it is moving in a circle. Pour the eggs into the broth in a slow, steady stream so that ribbons of coagulated egg form, about one minute.

HOT-AND-SOUR SOUP

At the outset, we knew we could expect three challenges when trying to make this soup in an American kitchen. First, we would need to find substitutes for a few hard-to-find ingredients. Second, we had to arrive at the correct balance of flavors. Hot-and-sour soup should be complex, with hot, spicy, and sour flavors most prominent. Third, we had to perfect the texture, which should be silky and thick.

We focused first on the hard-to-find ingredients, in particular wood ear fungus (a kind of mushroom) and lily buds (which come from tiger lilies), both of which have a chewy texture and earthy flavor. We found that dried shiitake mushrooms were the best substitute.

While dried shiitakes are a good visual replacement for wood ear fungus, the soup looked odd without the thin shredded bits of lily bud. As suggested in some sources, we tested both shredded leeks and bamboo shoots. Bamboo shoots seemed more authentic and were easier to prepare.

Almost every recipe we researched included chicken stock, soy sauce, vinegar, sesame oil, pepper, tofu, and egg. The type of vinegar and pepper used varied.

We tested distilled white, rice, white wine, and apple cider vinegars and found that mild rice vinegar provided the necessary sour notes without adding any distracting flavors. Chinese black vinegar (an ingredient available mostly in

Asian markets) is also often added for flavor and color. Some sources we consulted suggested using Worcestershire sauce as a substitute, and it worked beautifully, adding the dark color and complex, pungent flavor the soup needed.

We tested cayenne, white, and black pepper, alone and in combination. Cayenne was the testers' least favorite. It created a reddish color and an overpoweringly hot flavor. Black and white pepper were equally enjoyed. Since black pepper is a more common item, we chose it for our recipe.

The final issue that remained to be tested was thickening the soup. At this point, we knew that a liberal amount of cornstarch would be needed to create a thick broth. When we used just two or three tablespoons, the heavy ingredients in the soup (tofu, pork, and vegetables) fell to the bottom of the pot. In the end, we found that one-third cup of cornstarch is needed to thicken eight cups of broth.

The point at which the cornstarch is added is also important. When added after the acid (the rice vinegar), the cornstarch often failed to thicken the soup. Several food scientists we spoke to explained that because acid can prevent starch granules from bonding, it is preferable to add the acid after the cornstarch has dissolved and its granules bonded together to form the dense network that thickens the broth. Once the acid is added, the soup must not cook too long, or you again run the risk of causing the soup to thin out.

Hot-and-Sour Soup
serves 6 to 8

➤ N O T E : *If using canned broth, reduce the amount of soy sauce added to the vinegar mixture by 1 tablespoon.*

10	dried shiitake mushrooms
1½	cups hot water
1½	teaspoons dry sherry
1	tablespoon Asian sesame oil
3	tablespoons soy sauce
⅓	cup plus 1 teaspoon cornstarch
⅓	cup cool water
1	boneless center-cut pork chop (about 4 ounces and ½ inch thick), trimmed of fat
3	tablespoons rice vinegar
2	tablespoons Worcestershire sauce
1½	teaspoons ground black pepper
6	cups chicken stock
½	cup bamboo shoots, cut into ⅛-inch strips
½	pound firm tofu, drained and cut into strips 2 by ¼ inches
1	large egg, lightly beaten
2	tablespoons thinly sliced scallions

⁞ I N S T R U C T I O N S :

1. Place shiitakes in small bowl, cover with hot water, and

2 7

soak until softened, about 20 minutes. Carefully lift shiitake from water, letting grit stay on bottom of bowl. Trim and discard stems and slice caps into ⅛-inch strips. Strain soaking liquid through sieve lined with paper towel into large soup kettle. Set aside.

2. Mix sherry, 2 teaspoons sesame oil, 1 tablespoon soy sauce, and 1 teaspoon cornstarch together in small bowl. Slice meat crosswise against grain into thin strips about 1½ inches long. Toss pork with sherry marinade and set aside for at least 10 minutes.

3. Blend remaining ⅓ cup cornstarch with cool water in small bowl. Set aside, leaving a spoon in bowl. Combine remaining 2 tablespoons soy sauce with vinegar, Worcestershire, and pepper in another bowl and set aside.

4. Add stock to soup kettle with mushroom soaking liquid. Bring to a boil over medium heat. Reduce heat to a simmer and add mushrooms and bamboo shoots. Bring back to a simmer and cook for 4 minutes. Gently stir in tofu and pork, including marinade. Bring back to a simmer and cook 2 minutes.

5. Recombine cornstarch mixture and stir into simmering soup until it thickens, about 1 minute. Stir in vinegar mixture, then turn off heat. Without stirring soup, slowly drizzle egg in circular motion into pot. Gently stir once so egg forms into thin streamers and cooks completely, about 1 minute. Stir in remaining 1 teaspoon sesame oil. Ladle into bowls and garnish with scallions. Serve immediately.

chapter three

DUMPLINGS

THIN SHEETS OF PASTA CAN BE USED TO wrap any number of fillings for quick Asian dumplings. Our first question about dumplings concerned the wrapper. Is homemade better than store-bought? We made our own and found the process unbearably tedious. We also found that store-bought wrappers deliver better results. They are moisture-free and much easier to work with than homemade wrappers, which stuck to pots and cooked up gummy in our tests. Buying wrappers allows you to concentrate on making a filling and dipping sauce.

Wrappers, more specifically referred to as wonton wrappers or wonton skins, are delicate and paper-thin, usually about $1/32$ of an inch. They are typically packed in 3-inch squares and made from flour, eggs, and salt. Wonton wrappers are sold fresh in the refrigerator case and can be frozen for several months if not used in a week or so. If you decide to freeze them, do so in small batches, since they cannot be separated from each other until completely thawed and, once thawed, do not take well to refreezing. We found that wrappers will thaw to room temperature in an hour or two.

The quality of wrappers varies from brand to brand, and we found thickness to be the most important variable. Look for at least 50 wrappers per pound to make sure the skins you are buying are not too thick. Brands with fewer wrappers per pound will cook up thick and doughy.

Dumplings can be boiled, steamed, pan-fried, or deep-fried. Boiling allows the wrappers to absorb plenty of moisture and expand as they cook. It also keeps the exterior especially moist and tender and is the best choice if the dumplings are to be floated in a bowl of soup.

Steaming yields moist but resilient dumplings with chewy skins. Unlike boiling, we found that steaming does not dilute the flavors in the filling and is a better choice for protecting delicate ingredients. If making dumplings to serve as an appetizer, we prefer steaming to boiling.

We tested deep-frying and found that this method yields crisp, tasty dumplings with an appealing golden color.

And, because fried dumplings brown, they develop a natural sweetness from the caramelization, something that does not happen when dumplings are boiled or steamed. Of course, deep-frying dumplings is messy.

Somewhere between deep-frying and steaming is pan-frying, which combines two cooking methods and retains the advantages of both. The dumplings are first browned in hot oil in a skillet and then steamed to tenderness. We found it best to sauté them a second time, after they are steamed, to make sure the bottoms are nice and crisp. Pan-fried dumplings, also called potstickers, must have at least one flat side for browning.

With our cooking methods chosen, we focused on the shapes best suited to each. We also wanted to find shapes that were easy to assemble. Pyramids are ideal for pan-frying because they have a flat bottom that becomes crisp. Among similar shapes, we find they are the easiest to assemble.

Pyramids work well for steaming, but they take up a lot of room in the steamer basket. We wondered if a smaller shape would work as well. While the wonton shape seemed best for soup, it looked a little odd on an appetizer plate. The tortellini shape was appealing on two counts: its compact size makes it possible to fit many in a steamer basket at one time, and its shape stands up well to cooking and serving.

We tested three ways to seal dumplings—brushing the

edges with beaten egg, brushing the edges with water, and leaving the edges alone and hoping the dough would be tacky enough to seal on its own. We quickly discovered that dumplings need a moist sealant to keep them from opening up when cooked. Water was less messy than egg and worked beautifully; you can moisten the edges with your fingertip or a small brush.

Should you want to hold dumplings before serving, we found that they can sit refrigerated on a baking sheet for several hours. Line the baking sheet with parchment or wax paper, but don't try to flour the sheet; when we tried this, the flour made the dumplings gummy when cooked. And don't cover the baking sheet. When we covered it with plastic wrap, the wrappers got moist on the bottom and stuck to the tray. Although the uncovered dumplings dried out a bit, overall the results were better.

If you want to hold the dumplings for longer than a few hours, they must be frozen or will become soggy. Freeze the dumplings on a paper-lined baking sheet and then transfer them to an airtight container to prevent freezer burn. We found it best to cook frozen dumplings straight from the freezer. Add two to three minutes to the cooking time (pyramids will need the full three minutes).

Pan-Fried Dumplings
makes 32 dumplings, enough for 6 to 8 servings

➤ N O T E : *Pan-fried dumplings must lie flat on at least one side if they are to brown.*

1	cup canned low-sodium chicken broth or water
3	tablespoons vegetable oil
32	pyramid dumplings stuffed with any filling (see figures 5 and 6, page 35)
1	recipe Soy-Ginger Dipping Sauce or any variation (page 43)

I N S T R U C T I O N S :

1. Bring broth or water to a simmer in small saucepan.

2. Meanwhile, heat 2 tablespoons oil in large skillet over medium-high heat. When oil is hot and hazy, add half the dumplings, flat sides down. Fry until bottoms are brown, about 2 minutes. Add ½ cup simmering broth to skillet, pouring it around dumplings. Cover and cook until liquid is absorbed, about 3 minutes longer (add another 3 minutes if frozen). Uncover and let dumplings fry until bottoms are crisp again, about 1 minute. Serve immediately with dipping sauce on the side.

3. Heat remaining tablespoon of oil in empty skillet. Add remaining dumplings and repeat process, using remaining broth as directed. Serve immediately.

Figure 5.

*To make pyramid-shaped dumplings, place two level teaspoons of
filling in the center of a square wonton wrapper. Moisten the
edges lightly with water. Bring up two opposite corners of the
wrapper, and join them over the filling.*

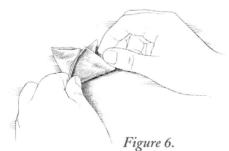

Figure 6.

*Holding the pinched corners together over the filling, bring up the
other two sides of the wrapper, one at a time, and pinch all four
sides together over the filling to make a point. Pinch the seams
firmly together to seal. Repeat with remaining filling and wrappers. A single filling recipe is enough to make about 32 pyramids.*

Steamed Dumplings

makes 32 dumplings, enough for 6 to 8 servings

➤ NOTE: *If you own a bamboo steamer basket, it can be used for this recipe. Simply grease the basket and arrange the dumplings inside. Bring water (it should be ¾ inch below the bottom of the basket) to a boil in a skillet large enough to hold the basket. Reduce to a simmer and set the covered basket in the skillet. Steam as directed. When the dumplings are done, place the basket on a plate, remove the cover, and serve.*

32   tortellini dumplings (see figures 7–9, pages 37–38) or pyramid dumplings (see figures 5–6, page 35)
        stuffed with any filling

1   recipe Soy-Ginger Dipping Sauce or any variation (page 43)

⁝ INSTRUCTIONS:

1. Grease a large collapsible steamer basket. Fill a large soup kettle with enough water to come ¾ inch below bottom of basket. Bring to a simmer over medium-low heat.

2. Arrange half of dumplings in basket, making sure they don't touch. Lower basket into kettle. Increase heat to high; cover and steam until dumplings are cooked through, about 5 minutes (add 2 to 3 minutes if frozen). Remove basket from kettle and serve dumplings immediately with dipping sauce.

3. Check water level in pot, adding more as necessary. Grease basket again and arrange remaining dumplings in basket, without letting them touch. Lower basket into kettle and cook as directed.

Figure 7.

To make tortellini-shaped dumplings, position a square wonton wrapper with one point facing you. Place one level teaspoon of filling in the center. Moisten edges lightly with water. Fold the wrapper in half to form a triangle. Press to seal the edges.

Figure 8.
Fold the long edge containing the filling over, leaving the top of
the triangle exposed by about half an inch.

Figure 9.
Moisten the top side of the left point of the triangle, then bring
the two points together, right over left, to overlap, away from the
tip of the triangle. Pinch the points together to seal the
dumpling. Repeat with remaining filling and wrappers. A single
filling recipe will yield 60 to 65 tortellini-shaped dumplings.
Unless you are making dumplings for a party, freeze half and
then steam them at a later date.

FILLINGS AND DIPPING SAUCE

No matter how they are cooked, dumplings, with their rather bland dough wrappers, benefit from tangy and savory dipping sauces. A well-seasoned filling is also essential.

After testing dozens of filling recipes, we looked through our notes and realized that tasters consistently preferred the same seasonings, even when the main ingredients in the filling changed. We eventually developed a basic flavoring recipe that could be used with meat, vegetables, or seafood.

The seasonings are fairly traditional—ginger, garlic, rice wine or dry sherry, soy sauce, sesame oil, sugar, salt, and scallions. Two ingredients merit discussion: egg white and cornstarch.

Dumpling fillings must be smooth, creamy, and firm. The smooth part is fairly simple to achieve—just make sure to chop ingredients fairly small. We found that adding the egg white helps the filling set up properly in a firm but creamy mass.

The cornstarch is added to control moisture. If there's too much liquid in the filling, dumplings will become soggy and may break apart even before they are cooked. (That's why we ended up salting vegetables such as cabbage before adding them to fillings.) The cornstarch absorbs any excess moisture and prevents wrappers from becoming mushy.

Flavoring Mixture for Dumplings

makes enough for one recipe of dumpling filling

1½	teaspoons minced fresh ginger
1	medium garlic clove, minced
1½	teaspoons dry sherry or rice wine
1	tablespoon soy sauce
1	teaspoon Asian sesame oil
½	teaspoon sugar
¼	teaspoon salt
2	tablespoons minced scallion greens
½	large egg white
1½	teaspoons cornstarch

I N S T R U C T I O N S :

Mix all ingredients in medium bowl.

Shrimp Filling

makes about 1¹/2 cups, enough for 32 pyramid
dumplings or 65 tortellini or wonton dumplings

➤ NOTE: *A little ground pork holds together a filling of chopped
shrimp and water chestnuts in this classic dumpling filling.*

6	ounces shelled raw shrimp, coarsely chopped
2	ounces ground pork
6	peeled water chestnuts (fresh or canned), minced
1	recipe Flavoring Mixture for Dumplings

■■ INSTRUCTIONS:

Mix all ingredients in a medium bowl. Refrigerate until ready
to make dumplings.

Pork Filling

makes about 1¹/2 cups, enough for 32 pyramid
dumplings or 65 tortellini or wonton dumplings

➤ NOTE: *A classic for wonton soup dumplings. Although pork
is traditional, ground chicken works quite well in its place.*

8	ounces ground pork
6	peeled water chestnuts (fresh or canned), minced
1	recipe Flavoring Mixture for Dumplings

■■ INSTRUCTIONS:

Mix all ingredients in medium bowl. Refrigerate until ready
to make dumplings.

41

Mixed Vegetable Filling

makes about 1¹/2 cups, enough for
32 pyramid dumplings or
65 tortellini or wonton dumplings

➤ **NOTE**: *Cabbage, carrots, and mushrooms make a colorful and almost fatfree dumpling filling. Because of its high water content, cabbage must be salted and pressed before being used in a dumpling filling.*

- ½   **medium napa cabbage, finely shredded (about 6 cups)**
- 1   **tablespoon salt**
- ¾   **cup grated carrot (about 1 large carrot)**
- 8   **dried shiitake mushrooms, rehydrated in 1 cup hot water until softened, strained (liquid reserved for another use), and chopped fine**
- 1   **recipe Flavoring Mixture for Dumplings, page 40**

:: INSTRUCTIONS:

Toss cabbage and salt together in colander; let stand until cabbage wilts, 15 to 20 minutes. Rinse cabbage; squeeze dry. Mix cabbage with remaining ingredients. Refrigerate until ready to make dumplings.

Soy-Ginger Dipping Sauce

makes about 1 cup

➤ **NOTE:** *This relatively mild sauce goes well with almost every dumpling filling imaginable.*

¼	cup soy sauce
¼	cup rice vinegar
2½	teaspoons sugar
¼	cup water
½	medium scallion, minced
2	teaspoons minced fresh ginger
½	teaspoon Asian sesame oil

INSTRUCTIONS:

Bring soy sauce, vinegar, sugar, and water to a boil in small saucepan over medium heat, stirring briefly, until sugar dissolves. Pour into a bowl; stir in the scallion, ginger, and sesame oil. Cool sauce to room temperature. (Can be covered and refrigerated for several days.)

VARIATIONS:

Mustard Soy-Ginger Dipping Sauce

Stir in 1 to 2 tablespoons prepared hot Chinese mustard along with scallion, ginger, and sesame oil.

Spicy Soy-Ginger Dipping Sauce

Stir in 1 to 2 tablespoons chili paste or 1 teaspoon chili oil along with scallions, ginger, and sesame oil.

chapter four

❊

STEAMED FISH

STEAMED WHOLE FISH IS A CHINESE DELI-
cacy. In the United States, though, whole
fish can be hard to find, and most cooks lack
the proper pot in which to steam one. We
wanted to adapt this technique for fillets, making sure to
retain the most prized qualities of a steamed whole fish:
moist, perfectly cooked flesh that is lightly seasoned to
enhance, but not overwhelm, the flavor of the fish.

We started our testing with salmon fillets and focused
on the issue of equipment. In our research, we identified a
number of possible steaming containers: a bamboo steamer,
a collapsible metal steamer basket, a pasta pot with perforated insert, a glass pie plate, and a ceramic dinner plate.

We started our tests with a pie plate and heatproof dinner plate with a lip, assuming most everyone would have one or the other at home. Typically, the marinated or seasoned fish is placed on a plate and the plate then set on a rack in a wok or wide pot. Moving the plates in and out of the rather cramped Dutch oven we were using was a challenge. Perhaps more important, we found that fish did not cook evenly on a pie plate, which does not allow the steam to penetrate evenly through the fillet.

We next tested a pasta pot with a perforated insert. Removing the cooked fillets from this pot was challenging as well because there is not enough room to maneuver a spatula under the fish.

We moved on to a collapsible metal steamer basket, which many cooks have in their kitchen, and it worked beautifully. We found that a large basket, preferably 11 inches or more across, is needed to hold four fish fillets. You might get away with a slightly smaller basket when steaming compact salmon fillets, but longer, thinner pieces will hang off the edge of the basket.

Sticking is the other major issue. Fillets placed directly on the metal are hard to remove when done. Coating the basket with nonstick cooking spray works, but many traditional Chinese recipes place the fish on leafy greens instead. We tested napa cabbage, spinach, green cabbage, iceberg lettuce, bok choy, and chard. Owing to their sturdiness, the napa and green cabbage leaves worked best. The other greens tended to collapse during steaming, making it harder to remove both the fish and the greens from the steamer.

If each fillet is placed on a separate leaf, it is very easy to simultaneously remove both cabbage and fillet from the basket. The cabbage adds a subtle flavor to the fish, provides a bed to hold the juices of a marinade or cooking sauce, and looks appealing when served under the fillet.

We next tested bamboo steamers. Typically, a set includes two steamers and a cover. We determined that using one steamer at a time ensures even cooking; foods cook at different rates in the top and bottom steamers when they are stacked. We tried placing the steamer in the bottom of a large stockpot, in the bottom of a wide, straight-sided skillet, and on top of a narrower stockpot. All three setups worked, but we preferred the narrow stockpot; you can put a lot of water in a narrow stockpot pot without worrying about the water touching the fish, and, because you can put a lot of water in the pot, you don't have to worry about the pot running dry.

Up until this point, we had been steaming salmon fillets. With our steaming equipment chosen, we moved on to other fish. We found the cabbage leaf to be even more helpful when steaming thin fillets and flaky fish. In the end, you can use this method to steam almost any fish you like. Our tasters especially liked the results when steaming cod and halibut, although thinner white-fleshed fish, such as flounder and snapper, can be used if you fold the thin tails under to prevent overcooking.

Our final set of tests involved flavorings. Many traditional recipes call for marinating the fish before steaming, and we found this to be beneficial. Fish marinated briefly before cooking (10 minutes was enough) tasted better than fish steamed plain and then seasoned.

We like the subtle sweetness of rice wine (it was preferred over sherry, which tasters found too strong for white-fleshed fish) balanced with some soy sauce. A little minced garlic and ginger were welcome. Scallions and fermented black beans are traditional flavorings for Chinese steamed fish, and we like to add them to the fish just before turning on the heat to preserve their texture and color.

Some final notes on safety. Steam is very hot and can burn. The safest way to put a collapsible basket in the pot is to bring the water to a boil, then briefly shut off the flame while lowering it in (the flame should also be off when you remove the basket). Use oven mitts or a folded dry kitchen towel to hold the basket as you put it in and take it out of the pot. When it's time to test the fish, lift the lid at an angle away from you to release steam, and don't stick your face in the pot.

♕
Master Recipe
Steamed Fish with Black Beans and Scallions
serves 4

➤ **NOTE:** *We found fillets to be easy to steam in a large collapsible steamer basket placed in a Dutch oven. If you use a traditional bamboo basket, place it on top of a narrow stockpot filled with simmering water and add about 2 minutes to the cooking time. Because it's easy to overcook the fish, check for doneness early. Although this recipe calls for thick salmon, cod, or halibut fillets, it can be modified to work with thin white fish such as flounder and snapper. Fold each fillet so that the tail is tucked under the wide end and steam for 4 to 5 minutes.*

- 2   tablespoons rice wine or dry sherry
- 1   tablespoon soy sauce
- 1   teaspoon Asian sesame oil
- 1   medium garlic clove, minced
- 1   tablespoon minced fresh ginger
- 4   salmon fillets or thick white fish fillets, such as halibut or cod (each 6 to 8 ounces and 1½ inches thick)
- ½   teaspoon salt
- 4   large napa or green cabbage leaves
- 1   tablespoon fermented black beans, chopped
- 2   tablespoons thinly sliced scallions

48

┇ INSTRUCTIONS:

1. Mix together rice wine, soy sauce, oil, garlic, and ginger in small bowl. Place fish in shallow glass or ceramic pan, sprinkle with salt, and then drizzle with rice wine mixture. Marinate for 10 to 15 minutes.

2. Meanwhile, fill Dutch oven with 1 inch of water. Place large collapsible steamer basket in pot and check to make sure there's about ¾ inch of space between water level and bottom of basket. Remove basket from pot and line with napa leaves (see figure 10, page 51).

3. Cover pot with tight-fitting lid and bring water to a boil over high heat. Place one fish fillet on each cabbage leaf. Drizzle marinade over fish, then sprinkle with black beans and scallions (see figure 11, page 51).

4. Briefly turn off burner and carefully lower steamer basket into pot, holding it with an oven mitt or folded kitchen towel. Cover tightly and turn heat back to high. Steam 6 to 7 minutes for medium-rare (good for salmon) or 7 to 8 minutes for medium. To check for doneness, lower heat and lift lid away from you to protect your face from the steam. Working quickly and using a long, thin knife, check to see if fillets are opaque throughout and flake easily. Cover again and steam longer if necessary.

5. When fish is done, turn off heat and carefully remove basket from pot using oven mitt or folded kitchen towel. To remove fish from basket, just slide cabbage leaves and fish together onto individual plates. Serve immediately.

VARIATIONS:

Steamed Fish with Garlic and Cilantro

If you can't buy fermented black beans, try this variation.

Follow master recipe, increasing garlic to 2 large cloves and omitting black beans and scallions. Proceed as directed. Just before serving, garnish each fillet with scant 1 teaspoon minced fresh cilantro leaves.

Steamed Fish with Sizzling Ginger and Scallions

Follow master recipe, marinating fish in rice wine, soy sauce, and 1½ tablespoons minced ginger (omit sesame oil and garlic). Omit black beans. Cut 2 scallions into 1½-inch lengths and then slice lengthwise into very thin strips. When fish is almost done steaming, heat 4 teaspoons Asian sesame oil and 2 teaspoons peanut oil in small skillet until almost smoking. Transfer steamed fish to individual plates and sprinkle with prepared scallions. Immediately pour a little hot oil over each fillet, standing back in case oil splatters. Serve immediately.

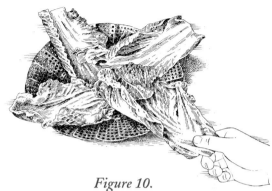

Figure 10.
*Line a large collapsible steamer basket with four napa cabbage
leaves, each slightly larger than a single piece of fish. Place leaves
so that the stalks face the edge of the basket and the leaves create
four distinct beds for the fish.*

Figure 11.
*Place one fish fillet on each cabbage leaf. Drizzle marinade over
fish and then sprinkle with black beans and scallions.*

51

chapter five

☂

KUNG PAO CHICKEN

KUNG PAO CHICKEN IS A RESTAURANT FAVORITE. Bits of silky chicken swim in a spicy, dark brown sauce along with peanuts and dried red chiles. Kung pao is not only spicy, it is rich. It typically contains few vegetables or none, making it uncharacteristic of most Chinese dishes. It should be served with plenty of rice to cut the heat and at least one vegetable dish to round out the meal. The biggest challenges when preparing kung pao are getting the texture of the chicken right and infusing the dish with enough—but not too much—heat.

The texture of the chicken in this dish is different from

52

that in a stir-fry. The exterior is an unusual combination of silky and crisp. In most restaurant kitchens, cooks obtain this crispiness by deep-frying (submerging the chicken in hot oil) and then draining the chicken. Chiles and aromatics are then stir-fried (cooked in a thin film of oil), and the sauce and chicken are added back at the end. We tested deep-frying as well as pan-frying (cooking the chicken in a shallow depth of oil) and got great results with pan-frying the chicken in just three tablespoons of oil. The oil is drained off after the chicken is cooked.

Pan-frying (or deep-frying in restaurants) is what gives the chicken its crisp crust, but the desired silkiness comes from the marinade. Some sources suggest "velveting" the chicken in egg white; others add some cornstarch and/or oil to the marinade.

We tested velveting first, adding egg whites and cornstarch to a simple rice wine and soy sauce marinade. We prepared a second batch with cornstarch alone added to the rice wine and soy sauce. For the third batch, we included neither cornstarch nor egg white.

Tasters agreed that adding cornstarch to the marinade was a good idea. It gave the chicken the silky, tender texture we wanted. Egg white and cornstarch performed on a par with the cornstarch-only mixture, so we opted to omit the egg white. We had also seen recipes that called for a little oil. We tried this tip and found that oil helps to keep the chicken pieces separate when cooked, which in turn improves the texture of the meat.

Until this point in the testing, we had been cooking diced chicken breasts with good results. We wondered how chicken thighs would do. Tasters felt that the thighs were even better—meatier, juicier, and more flavorful.

Chicken is traditionally diced for kung pao; tasters preferred a small ½-inch dice. We found that one pound of diced chicken could be comfortably cooked in a 12-inch skillet. Add any more chicken and it has to be cooked in batches to ensure that it will brown well and not stew in its own juices. Given the waste associated with chicken thighs (they contain a fair amount of fat that should be trimmed), we decided to buy 1¼ pounds of chicken to yield the pound needed for the recipe.

With the chicken element under control, we turned our attention to the heat level. Traditionally, kung pao chicken comes to the table filled with toasted dried red chiles. To release the flavor and heat from the chiles, we found it is necessary to break them in half before toasting them in the oil. Most of the heat in a chile pepper is found in the seeds and interior ribbing, not the outer shell.

Because dried red chiles are sometimes not easy to come by, we wondered if hot red pepper flakes could be used instead. While toasting dried chiles in oil releases their flavor, pepper flakes tasted burned when cooked this way. We found it better to add them with the aromatics (garlic, ginger, and scallions) toward the end of the cooking time.

Tasters felt that kung pao chicken made with hot red pepper flakes instead of dried chiles looked a bit odd. We found that adding some diced red bell pepper helped solved this problem. The charred bits of bell pepper add some visual contrast that the chicken needs. Their sweetness is also a good foil for the rich, spicy flavors in this dish.

In the end, tasters preferred the heat given by the dried red chiles. They seemed to have a fuller flavor than the pepper flakes, which were merely spicy. Because of the way the dried chiles are cooked, the flavor permeates the dish and blends with its sweet, sour, and salty elements. Hot red pepper flakes stand out. You taste heat, then the sweet, sour, and salty flavors. It's not that the hot red pepper flakes are bad; they just aren't as good.

Our next challenge was to assemble the elements of the sauce. Kung pao has a complex, brown sauce with strong sweet and sour notes to balance the heat of the chiles. Chicken broth, soy sauce, rice wine, and vinegar were pretty much standard in the recipes we consulted. We found that too much vinegar made the sauce harsh. A good deal of sweetness was also essential. In recipes that called for little or no sugar, the

55

heat was one-dimensional. We found that a full tablespoon of sugar is best.

Because cornstarch generally makes stir-fry sauces too thick, we tend to shy away from it. However, the ingredients in kung pao—diced chicken, diced red bell pepper, and peanuts—are so smooth that the sauce was not adhering properly. We tried reducing the sauce before adding the cooked chicken back to the pan. This helped, but the sauce was still pooling. We found that just ½ teaspoon of corn starch solved this problem. Any more cornstarch—even just an extra ½ teaspoon—turns the sauce gummy, so measure carefully.

The aromatic elements (garlic, ginger, and scallions) were fairly easy to incorporate. Tasters liked more scallions in this dish for contrast with the chicken and peanut flavors. Cutting scallions into ½-inch lengths rather than mincing made them seem more like a vegetable and helped to maintain freshness, a quality otherwise missing from this dish.

We tried other vegetables—mushrooms, water chestnuts, and celery—but tasters consistently preferred a streamlined dish of just chicken, diced red bell pepper, and peanuts. One final note: Use a nonstick skillet. If you don't, plan on adding more oil to keep the chicken from sticking.

Master Recipe

Kung Pao Chicken

serves 4

➤ NOTE: *If you have small dried red chiles on hand, use them instead of the hot red pepper flakes. For a medium-hot flavor, cook 5 to 10 chiles with the bell pepper, adding an extra tablespoon of oil so the chiles don't scorch. Crack a couple of the chiles in half to release the seeds, or open all of the chiles for a superspicy dish. Make sure not to eat the chiles. If you prefer, substitute 1 pound of boneless, skinless chicken breasts for the thighs. Serve with plenty of Sticky White Rice (page 72) to cut the heat.*

3	tablespoons soy sauce
2½	tablespoons rice wine or dry sherry
1	tablespoon plus ½ teaspoon cornstarch
1¼	pounds skinless, boneless chicken thighs, trimmed of fat and cut into ½-inch cubes
5	tablespoons plus 1 teaspoon peanut oil
3	tablespoons canned chicken broth
1	tablespoon sugar
1	teaspoon rice vinegar
1	teaspoon Asian sesame oil
1	small red bell pepper, cored, seeded, and cut into ½-inch dice

(Ingredients continued on next page)

5 7

(Ingredients continued from previous page)

- **2   large garlic cloves, minced**
- **1   tablespoon minced fresh ginger**
- **6   medium scallions, whites only, cut into ½-inch lengths**
- **1   teaspoon hot red pepper flakes, or to taste**
- **½   cup dry roasted, unsalted peanuts**

■■ INSTRUCTIONS:

1. Mix 1½ tablespoons soy sauce, 1½ tablespoons rice wine, and 1 tablespoon cornstarch together in medium bowl. Add chicken and toss. Add 1 tablespoon peanut oil and toss again. Set aside for 20 minutes.

2. Mix remaining 1½ tablespoons soy sauce, 1 tablespoon rice wine, and ½ teaspoon cornstarch together in small bowl. Stir in broth, sugar, vinegar, and sesame oil; set sauce aside.

3. Heat a 12- or 14-inch nonstick skillet over high heat for 3 minutes. Add 3 tablespoons peanut oil and swirl oil so that it evenly coats bottom of pan. Heat oil until it just starts to shimmer and smoke. Add chicken and stir-fry until seared and three-quarters cooked, about 2 minutes. Strain chicken into clean bowl and set aside. Carefully wipe out pan with paper towel.

4. Put pan back over high heat and let it come up to temperature, 1 minute. When hot, add 1 tablespoon peanut oil and swirl oil so that it evenly coats bottom of pan. When oil just starts to smoke, add bell pepper and stir-fry for 1 minute. Clear center of pan and add garlic, ginger, scallions, and pepper flakes, drizzle with remaining teaspoon peanut oil, and stir-fry until fragrant, 10 to 15 seconds.

5. Add sauce and cook, stirring constantly, until it boils, 5 to 10 seconds. Add chicken back to pan and stir-fry until ingredients are well coated with sauce and sizzling hot, about 1 minute. Stir in peanuts and serve immediately.

VARIATION:
Kung Pao Shrimp
Even if pan-fried, shrimp never develops the silky crust found on chicken, so it's best to stir-fry the shrimp in a film of oil.

Follow master recipe, replacing chicken with 1 pound small or medium shrimp, peeled, and eliminating 1 tablespoon cornstarch and 1 tablespoon oil from marinade in step 1. Reduce amount of oil in step 3 to 1 tablespoon. Cook shrimp until bright pink, 1 to 1½ minutes. Transfer shrimp to bowl and proceed as directed.

chapter six

BEEF & BROCCOLI IN GARLIC SAUCE

O UR FOREMOST CONCERN WHEN DEVELOP-ing a recipe for beef and broccoli in garlic sauce was the beef. Too often gray, soggy, and/or tough, the beef in this popular dish should be well browned and tender.

Our second area of concern was the broccoli. The florets should be bright green and crisp-tender. Most recipes steam or blanch florets in a separate pot to avoid overcooking. This seemed like a cumbersome step to us; we wanted to simplify the process without sacrificing quality.

Finally, the sauce can be problematic. Sometimes the gar-lic flavor is too harsh; other times it is too mild. We wanted to figure out how much garlic to add, when to add it, and what other ingredients would complement rather than overwhelm the sweet garlic flavor of the sauce.

Although some sources suggest cuts from the shoulder and round, flank steak is the most common choice for stir-frying. After some testing, we found flank steak to have the best combination of beefy flavor and tenderness. Round was dry and tough, and the shoulder was too chewy.

The biggest challenge when cooking flank steak is dealing with all the liquid that it sheds in the skillet. Our tests showed that ¾ pound of thin-sliced flank steak loses between ¼ cup and ⅓ cup of its juices. The danger is that the beef will stew in these juices rather than sear. We found that the combination of using a hot pan and cooking in batches got the beef in and out of the skillet quickly and kept the meat from developing a stewed flavor.

The juices continue to leach out of the meat even after it comes out of the pan. We noticed that meat that had been delicious fresh from the skillet turned soggy several minutes later. Putting the beef in a strainer after stir-frying solved this problem, separating the juices from the meat. This juice can be added back to the pan along with the meat to give the dish a more beefy flavor.

The tried-and-true method of blanching the broccoli in a separate pot and then adding it to the stir-fry along with the sauce worked well for us, but we wanted to avoid the hassle of dirtying another pot. We tried stir-frying the broccoli, adding the sauce (but not the meat), and then covering the pan. This method was very imprecise. The broccoli tended to overcook and the sauce to overreduce.

We had better luck when we stir-fried the broccoli in the skillet after the beef had been cooked. (The skillet was empty at this point.) After a quick stir-fry, we added a little water, covered the pan, and then steamed the broccoli. We found that two minutes of covered cooking delivered perfectly cooked broccoli. When we piled the broccoli into a bowl, the residual heat caused the florets to soften further. To keep our broccoli crisp-tender, we found it best to spread the broccoli out on a plate covered with a clean towel, which absorbed excess moisture.

It always seems such as waste to throw out the broccoli stems, especially for a stir-fry. We found that stems would cook in the same time as florets if peeled and cut on the diagonal into 1-inch rounds about ⅛ inch thick.

Although beef and broccoli is an admirable combination, most tasters felt that the addition of another vegetable would make the dish more visually and texturally appealing. In the end, we liked red bell pepper for its crunch and color.

We now turned our attention to the sauce. Some recipes add the garlic directly to the sauce. Tasters felt that garlic added this way was too raw-tasting. We had better results stir-frying the garlic along with the scallions and ginger. Doubling the usual amount of garlic for a stir-fry (from 1 to 2 tablespoons) gave us the deep, rich garlic flavor we wanted.

Several other possible contributors to the sauce were rejected by our panel of tasters: sugar for making the stir-fry too sweet, vinegar and sherry for adding unwelcome harsh notes, and hot red pepper flakes for competing with the garlic flavor. One additional ingredient, however, proved to be key: oyster sauce, the flavor of which goes extremely well with beef and broccoli. Oyster sauce provides body and color, and the complexity of its flavor eliminates the need for most other sauce ingredients. Only chicken broth, soy sauce, and sesame oil were needed to turn oyster sauce into a complete stir-fry sauce.

♛

Master Recipe

Beef and Broccoli in Garlic Sauce

serves 4

➤ **NOTE**: *After cooking the beef, steam the broccoli in the same skillet over medium heat. When the broccoli is tender but still crisp, remove it to a plate to prevent further cooking. Turn the heat back to high and finish this dish in a sizzling hot skillet.*

¾	pound flank steak, boneless, trimmed of fat and sliced thin (see figures 12 and 13, pages 67 and 68)
1½	tablespoons soy sauce
1	tablespoon dry sherry or rice wine
3	tablespoons oyster sauce
2	tablespoons canned chicken broth
1	teaspoon Asian sesame oil
5	tablespoons peanut oil
1¼	pounds broccoli, florets broken into bite-sized pieces; stems trimmed, peeled, and cut on diagonal into 1-inch rounds, about ⅛ inch thick
⅓	cup water
1	small red bell pepper, cored, seeded, and diced
2	tablespoons minced garlic
1	tablespoon minced fresh ginger
2	tablespoons scallions, whites only, cut into ½-inch lengths

1. Toss beef with 1 tablespoon soy sauce and dry sherry in medium bowl; set aside, tossing once or twice.

2. Mix remaining ½ tablespoon soy sauce with oyster sauce, chicken broth, and sesame oil in small bowl; set aside.

3. Heat a 12- or 14-inch nonstick skillet over high heat for 3 minutes. Drain beef. Add 1 tablespoon peanut oil to pan and swirl so oil coats bottom of pan evenly. Heat oil until it just starts to shimmer and smoke. Add half the beef and stir-fry until seared and three-quarters cooked, about 1 minute. Transfer beef to strainer set over clean bowl to keep cooked meat and juices separate. Repeat process with another tablespoon of oil and second batch of beef.

4. Let pan come back up to temperature, about 1 minute. When hot, add 1 tablespoon oil and swirl so oil coats bottom of pan evenly. When oil just starts to smoke, add broccoli and stir-fry for 30 seconds. Add water, cover pan, and lower to medium heat. Steam broccoli until crisp-tender, about 2 minutes. Transfer broccoli to plate lined with clean kitchen towel.

5. Let the pan come up to temperature, about 1 minute. When hot, add 1 tablespoon oil and swirl oil so that it coats bottom of pan evenly. When oil just starts to smoke, add bell pepper and stir-fry for 1 minute. Clear center of pan and add garlic, ginger, and scallions, drizzle with remaining tablespoon of oil, and stir-fry until fragrant but not colored, 10 to 15 seconds. Add broccoli back to pan and stir scallions, garlic, and ginger into vegetables for 20 seconds off heat.

6. Add cooked beef and its liquid, stir in sauce, and stir-fry until ingredients are well coated with sauce and sizzling hot, about 1 minute. Serve immediately.

VARIATIONS:

Scallops and Broccoli in Garlic Sauce

To achieve a nicely browned exterior, turn scallops only once while stir-frying.

Follow master recipe, substituting ¾ pound large sea scallops, tendons removed and cut in half through the equator, for flank steak. Reduce amount of soy sauce to 1 tablespoon and use it all in step 2. Omit step 1 (scallops do not need to be marinated) and sherry. Stir-fry scallops in two batches according to step 3 until opaque, 40 to 60 seconds. Proceed as directed.

Bok Choy in Garlic Sauce

Follow master recipe, omitting beef, broccoli, and bell pepper. Prepare bok choy as directed in figures 14 through 16 (see pages 68–69). Reduce amount of soy sauce to 1 table-

6 6

spoon and use it all in step 2. Omit step 1 (bok choy does not need to be marinated) and sherry. Stir-fry bok choy whites in two batches according to step 3 until crisp-tender, 1 to 2 minutes, and remove from pan. Omit step 4. Substitute bok choy leaves for bell pepper in step 5, adding 1 tablespoon water with leaves and reducing cooking time to 30 seconds. Cook garlic, ginger, and scallions as directed. Add stalks back to pan; stir for 20 seconds off heat. Stir in sauce, stir-fry for 30 seconds, and serve immediately.

Figure 12.
Slice partially frozen flank steak into pieces 2 inches wide.

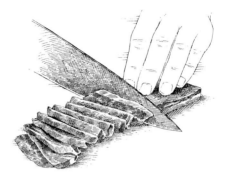

Figure 13.
Cut each piece of flank steak against the grain into very thin slices.

Figure 14.
Cut the leafy green portions of the bok choy away from the stalk.

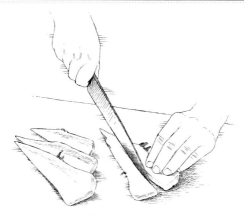

Figure 15.
Cut each stalk in half lengthwise and then crosswise
into strips ½ inch wide.

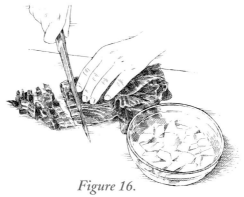

Figure 16.
Stack the leafy greens and then slice them crosswise into thin
strips. Keep the sliced stalks and leaves separate.

6 9

chapter seven

ဒ

RICE

A S A SIDE DISH, RICE HELPS STRETCH OUT small portions of highly seasoned stir-fries. Rice can also take center stage when served as a seasoned side dish or light entrée. This chapter examines how to cook plain white rice, Chinese style, as well as how to turn leftover rice into fried rice.

STICKY WHITE RICE

In China (and much of Asia), rice is cooked so that the texture is sticky and the grains clump together. This texture is well suited to eating with chopsticks.

While many cooks assume that Chinese restaurants use a special kind of rice, they do not. Long-grain rice will cook up fluffy or sticky depending on how it is prepared. In Western recipes, once the rice and water come to a boil, the pan is covered and the rice is cooked over low heat. In most Chinese recipes, the rice and water are cooked uncovered until the water level drops below the surface of the rice and small holes form on the surface. At this point, the heat is reduced and the rice finishes cooking in much the same manner as in Western recipes.

The differences in technique have several consequences. It generally takes about 10 minutes of active boiling for the water level to drop down below the surface of the rice. During this period, the rice is subjected to constant agitation and thus releases more starch. In addition, because the pot is uncovered, water is evaporating, so less water is left in the pot once it is covered.

Our research presented us with two variables for testing: whether or not to rinse the rice before cooking and what should be the ratio of rice to water. While rice is rinsed in many cultures for health reasons, the rice in the United States is quite clean. That said, we wondered if rinsing had some other benefit. The answer is no. We found that rinsed rice cooked up a tad fluffier than unrinsed rice, which is fine for a pilaf but not recommended when making rice to accompany a Chinese meal. As for the ratio of water to rice, we found that a ratio of 1 cup rice to 1½ cups water worked perfectly.

Sticky White Rice

makes about 6 cups, serving 4 to 6

➤ **NOTE:** *This traditional Chinese cooking method yields sticky rice that is easy to eat with chopsticks. This rice closely resembles the plain white rice served at most Chinese restaurants.*

2	**cups long-grain rice**
3	**cups water**
½	**teaspoon salt**

INSTRUCTIONS:

1. Place rice, water, and salt in medium saucepan set over medium-high heat. Bring water to a boil. Cook, uncovered, until water level drops below top surface of rice and small holes form in rice, about 10 minutes.

2. Reduce heat to very low, cover, and cook until rice is tender, about 15 minutes longer. Rice is best served immediately, but pan can be taken off heat and set aside, covered, for up to 15 minutes.

FRIED RICE

Fried rice is a Chinese-American restaurant classic. It's also a dish frequently made at home in China. While both traditions start with leftover rice, they depart in their perspective on soy sauce. Fried rice in China is rarely made with soy sauce, while American restaurant versions often contain so much soy sauce that the rice is dyed brown. In addition to cooking questions—such as the temperature of the rice before frying it, the amount of oil, and the type of pan—we wanted to resolve the flavor issues that we uncovered in our research.

Fried rice should contain separate grains of firm but tender rice. We wondered what would be the best initial temperature for the rice—freshly warm from the pot, room temperature, or cold?

Freshly made rice produced the least desirable results. The individual grains did not separate, and they were overly tender and mushy. Room-temperature rice was only slightly better. Some grains separated, but overall the rice was still too soft and clumpy. Cold rice worked best in our tests.

Some sources suggest refrigerating the rice in a bowl. Others call for spreading it out on a tray for rapid cooling. The rice is then refrigerated.

We found that spreading the rice out on a baking sheet allows it to dry more quickly and better preserves its flavor

73

and texture. Rice cooled in a bowl was stickier and less flavorful. The next day out of the refrigerator it did not feel as dry as rice that had been stored on a baking sheet. We did notice that rice cooled on a metal baking sheet could be stained brown from rust on the pan. Lining the pan with a clean kitchen towel prevents any discoloration. We also found that the towel absorbs moisture, which also creates more desirable dry rice. Rice stored this way is best used between 24 and 48 hours after cooking. It's also important to cover rice left this long in the refrigerator to keep it from picking up off flavors from other foods.

As an aside, we tested rice stored in a quart container from a Chinese restaurant. We had excellent results when we used this rice the next day. Our theory is that the standard heavyweight paper Chinese food container allows some air to penetrate into the rice, which facilitates its drying. At the same time, the container prevents the rice from picking up that hard-to-describe refrigerator taste.

With the preparation of the rice decided, it was time to start testing the frying process. The main issues were the type of pan (nonstick or conventional) and the type and quantity of oil.

A nonstick skillet consistently produced the best results. When using a regular skillet, more oil is needed, and even with more oil the egg (used in most fried rice recipes) may stick. If using a regular skillet, it's best to clean the pan after removing the egg and before continuing with the recipe.

Tests showed that even when using a nonstick skillet a substantial amount of oil is required. Oil is needed to scramble the egg, to cook the protein (we include recipes that use pork, chicken, or shrimp), and to cook and coat the vegetables. We ended up using close to ¼ cup of oil, depending on the components of the dish. If you skimp on the oil, the texture of the dish suffers, sticking is likely, and the rice will be mushy.

We next turned to the issue of seasonings. Although soy sauce is the most obvious seasoning in the fried rice prepared at Chinese-American restaurants, we found that salt enlivens fried rice without overpowering other ingredients. We decided to make salt part of the master recipe and leave soy for a variation. Sesame oil, ginger, and curry are examples of seasonings that, when used in moderation, create interesting and flavorful variations; none of these was listed as an ingredient in the basic fried rice recipes we reviewed.

The final issue concerned the other main ingredients in fried rice—namely, egg, vegetables, and proteins.

Eggs are a must. To make sure the egg is perfectly cooked, we found it best to cook it first and to remove it from the pan before cooking the other ingredients. The technique of scrambling it over medium heat, using a wooden spatula to break it into small pieces, and cooking it until golden and aromatic yields pieces that will be flavorful and evenly distributed in the rice.

For a basic stir-fry, the choice of vegetables is simple. Tradition calls for scallions, peas, and sprouts, and we liked all of these ingredients. It took more time to figure out the order in which to add the rice and vegetables to the pan. When cooked first in oil by itself, the rice came out beautifully, each grain separate and the texture perfect. When the vegetables were added, though, the moisture they gave off caused the rice to soften and clump. We were surprised to learn that it's best to cook the vegetables first in a good amount of oil, which in turn lubricates the rice and facilitates a pleasing texture of all ingredients.

Our basic recipe contains only egg for protein. Most Americans will prefer one of the heartier variations made with shrimp, chicken, or pork. We found that raw protein, such as shrimp or scallops, is best cooked before the egg and then removed from the pan. The protein can be added back to the rice later, along with the cooked egg.

Although you can cook protein for the purpose of using it in fried rice, the beauty of this dish is its capacity for leftovers. For best results when using cooked protein, treat it like a vegetable. The protein and the rice will then be coated with oil and have the most pleasing texture.

☙

Master Recipe
Fried Rice
serves 4

➤ **NOTE:** *In China, soy sauce is never used in fried rice. This master recipe is authentic in being delicately flavored with salt. The rice remains white, and the other ingredients are vibrant and fresh tasting. Try the pork variation for a more American rendition; it includes soy, which flavors and colors the rice. Although we recommend that you cool and store the rice as directed below, you can use leftover rice that has been stored in an airtight container. It will cook up mushier and with more clumps than rice cooled on a towel-lined baking sheet.*

5	cups cooked white rice, cooled to room temperature on towel-lined baking sheet, covered, and refrigerated
3½	tablespoons peanut oil
2	large eggs, lightly beaten
4	medium scallions, thinly sliced
1	cup frozen peas, thawed
1	teaspoon salt
1	cup mung bean sprouts

⊞ **INSTRUCTIONS:**

1. Separate rice with fingers to break up large clumps.

2. Heat a 12- or 14-inch nonstick skillet over medium heat

77

for 2 minutes. Add 1½ tablespoons oil and swirl so that it coats bottom of pan evenly. Add eggs and cook until lightly set; then use a wooden or heatproof plastic spatula to scramble and break into small pieces. Cook until eggs are light golden brown and aromatic, about 3 minutes. Scrape eggs into bowl and set aside.

3. Raise heat to high and let pan come back up to temperature, 1 to 2 minutes. When hot, add remaining 2 tablespoons oil and swirl to coat bottom of pan evenly. Add scallions and peas and stir-fry for 1 minute. Add rice and salt. Use spatula to break up any lumps and stir-fry until rice is hot, about 3 minutes. Add sprouts and eggs, mix well to blend, and heat through, about 1 minute. Serve immediately.

:: VARIATIONS:

Pork Fried Rice

Mix together 1½ tablespoons soy sauce, 1 tablespoon rice wine, and 1 teaspoon Asian sesame oil in small bowl and set aside. Follow master recipe through step 2. Heat pan as directed in step 3 and add 1 tablespoon peanut oil. Stir-fry 4 ounces finely diced cooked pork or ham for 1 minute. Add 1½ tablespoons more oil and continue with recipe. Omit salt and add soy mixture with eggs and sprouts.

Shrimp Fried Rice

Toss ½ pound small, peeled shrimp with 1 tablespoon rice wine, 1 teaspoon Asian sesame oil, 1 teaspoon minced fresh ginger, and ½ teaspoon soy sauce in medium bowl. Set aside for 15 minutes, tossing once or twice. Before cooking eggs, heat 1 tablespoon peanut oil over medium-high heat in skillet. Add shrimp and cook until bright pink, 1 to 2 minutes. Transfer cooked shrimp and all liquid to clean bowl and wipe out skillet with paper towel. Heat 1½ tablespoons more oil in empty skillet, cook egg, and proceed with master recipe as directed. Add shrimp back to pan with eggs in step 3.

Curried Chicken Fried Rice

Omit eggs and scallions in master recipe. Finely dice 1 medium onion, 1 small red bell pepper, and 4 ounces cooked chicken. Heat pan as directed. Add 2 tablespoons peanut oil and stir-fry onion over high heat until softened, about 2 minutes. Add peppers and cook for 2 minutes more. Add 2 teaspoons curry powder; stir-fry for 10 seconds or until fragrant. Add 1 tablespoon more peanut oil along with chicken and stir-fry for 1 minute. Add peas and continue with master recipe.

chapter eight

NOODLES

RESH CHINESE EGG NOODLES ARE SIMILAR TO fresh Italian pasta. Both are bright yellow and made with eggs and wheat. Chinese noodles are made with a different kind of wheat flour that yields firmer noodles when cooked. Chinese egg noodles are often round, not flat. They can be boiled and then either stir-fried to make lo mein or chilled and sauced to make cold sesame noodles.

LO MEIN

When lo mein is good, the noodles are well seasoned and slippery but not greasy. The bits of vegetable and protein add interest but do not overwhelm the noodles. Just as often, though, lo mein is oily or the sauce is one-dimensional. Our goals were simple: figure out how to deal with the noodles (what kind, how to cook, how to drain and rinse, how to stir-fry) and then determine how to add flavor through the sauce.

Because lo mein noodles should be separate and soft, we thought it might be necessary to boil them past the al dente stage. But noodles boiled too long became mushy when stir-fried. In the end, we had better luck with noodles boiled just short of al dente. The noodles finish cooking while being stir-fried.

So how long should you cook noodles destined for use in lo mein? Because the time required to cook until not quite tender differs depending on the type of noodle, we found it best to taste the noodles and stop the cooking process 30 seconds to 1 minute before they reached al dente. The quickest and easiest way to stop cooking is to rinse the drained noodles under cold running water. This also washes off extra starch.

Next we wanted to find out if there is an advantage to tossing the rinsed noodles in oil. As it turned out, there are two. First, it helps to keep the noodles from sticking together before stir-frying—an issue that becomes more problematic the longer the noodles are held. (Our tests showed that noodles could be held in the refrigerator for up to a day before stir-frying.) Second, the oil enhances the flavor and texture of the finished dish. We had seen recipes that called for peanut and sesame oil. In our tests, we preferred sesame oil for its more potent flavor.

Up until this point, we had been using fresh Chinese egg noodles. As expected, frozen Chinese egg noodles worked fine as long as we took the noodles straight from the freezer (defrosting caused them to stick together and become gummy) and added two minutes to the cooking time.

Since many home cooks don't have access to fresh Chinese noodles, we wanted to find an alternative. The dried Chinese noodles sold in many supermarkets were terrible. Tasters found these noodles to be too thin for use in lo mein and their texture overly soft.

Dried Italian pasta was not much better. When cooked until al dente, the noodles were much too springy for use in lo mein. They were chewy rather than soft. Overcooking helped somewhat, but this was an imperfect solution.

Fresh Italian pasta, bought at the supermarket, produced much better results. In fact, lo mein made with Contadina fresh linguine was praised by tasters. It was much softer than dried pasta, and its bright color was more authentic. We tried fresh spaghetti but found that the thicker, flatter linguine noodle worked (and looked) best.

With the noodle component of the dish under control, we moved on to the issue of the sauce. Our goal was to use minimal ingredients to get maximum flavor. Color was another important consideration, as tasters expressed a preference for lo mein with a rich, dark brown color.

Chicken broth and shiitake mushroom soaking liquid worked equally well as the primary liquid in the sauce and added subtle flavor. In terms of convenience, chicken broth is the logical choice for the master recipe and all variations with animal protein. Shiitake soaking liquid is perfect for vegetarian lo mein, where the mushrooms add a much-needed chewy, meaty texture.

Soy sauce is a must for flavor, color, and authenticity. Many sources suggested using a thick, reduced, sweetened soy sauce product. While we liked thick soy sauce for its effect on color, the strong, salty but sweet flavor it contributed was not well liked.

Oyster sauce was another matter. As with the thick soy sauce, just two tablespoons colored the noodles beautifully. This time, though, tasters loved the flavor.

Pork is the most common protein used in lo mein (although other proteins work well). We found slightly fattier meat to be preferable. Meat from a pork chop was better than tenderloin.

♛

Master Recipe

Pork Lo Mein

serves 4

➤   **N O T E : :** *Noodles tossed with some vegetables and protein make a delicious side dish for a more involved meal or a quick entrée for a weeknight supper. The key is to slightly undercook the noodles when they are first boiled and to cut the vegetables into thin strips. If fresh Chinese noodles are not available, substitute fresh Italian linguine and cook it for 1 to 2 minutes. Chopsticks or tongs (be careful not to scratch the pan bottom) help to combine the noodles with the other ingredients. Simply lift the noodles high off the pan, blending the components as you do so.*

1	tablespoon salt
¾	pound fresh Chinese egg noodles
1½	tablespoons Asian sesame oil
1	tablespoon dry sherry
2	tablespoons soy sauce
2	center-cut boneless pork chops (about 4 ounces each and ½ inch thick, fat trimmed)
¼	cup canned chicken broth
2	tablespoons oyster sauce
3	tablespoons peanut oil
1	small carrot, grated (about ½ cup)
¼	small head napa cabbage, cored and shredded (about 2 cups)

84

4   scallions, greens only, cut into 1-inch pieces
1   tablespoon minced fresh ginger
1   medium garlic clove, minced
1   cup mung bean sprouts

⠿ I N S T R U C T I O N S :

1. Bring 6 quarts water to a boil in large pot. Add salt and noodles, stir to separate, and cook until noodles are slightly underdone, 2 to 3 minutes. Drain thoroughly, rinse in cold water, and drain again. Toss noodles with sesame oil in large bowl. (Noodles can be covered and refrigerated for up to 1 day.)

2. Mix sherry and 1 tablespoon soy sauce together in small bowl. Slice meat crosswise against the grain into thin strips about 1½ inches long. Place in bowl and marinate for at least 10 minutes.

3. Mix chicken broth with oyster sauce and remaining tablespoon soy sauce in small bowl; set aside.

4. Heat a 12- or 14-inch nonstick skillet over high heat for 3 minutes. Add 1 tablespoon peanut oil and swirl so that oil coats bottom of pan evenly. Add pork and stir-fry until seared and three-quarters cooked, about 2 minutes. Scrape pork and all liquid into clean bowl, cover, and set aside. Carefully wipe out skillet with paper towel.

5. Let pan come back up to temperature, 1 to 2 minutes. When hot, add 1 tablespoon oil and swirl to coat bottom of pan evenly. Add carrot and cabbage and stir-fry until wilted, 1 to 2 minutes. Clear center of pan and add scallions, ginger, garlic, and remaining tablespoon of oil. Cook until fragrant, about 10 seconds, stir into the vegetables, and stir-fry 20 seconds off heat.

6. Add noodles, pork, sprouts, and chicken broth mixture to pan. Stir-fry and toss to combine all ingredients until noodles are heated through, 1 to 2 minutes. Serve immediately.

▪▪ **V A R I A T I O N S :**

Beef and Pepper Lo Mein

Follow master recipe, substituting 8 ounces flank steak, cut into thin strips (see figures 12 and 13, pages 67–68), for pork. Reduce stir-frying time in step 4 to 1 minute and place cooked steak in strainer to drain off excess juice. Replace carrot with ½ small red bell pepper cut into thin strips.

Shrimp and Snow Pea Lo Mein

Follow master recipe, substituting 8 ounces small, peeled shrimp for pork. Reduce stir-frying time in step 4 to 1 to 2 minutes. Replace carrot with 24 snow peas, ends and strings trimmed.

Vegetable Lo Mein

Place 8 dried shiitake mushrooms in small bowl, cover with hot water, and soak until softened, about 20 minutes. Carefully lift shiitake from water, leaving the grit in the bottom of the bowl. Pour off ¼ cup of soaking liquid and substitute for chicken broth in master recipe. Trim and discard mushroom stems and slice caps into ⅛-inch strips. Prepare master recipe, omitting pork and all of step 2, including sherry. Add an extra tablespoon of soy to mushroom liquid mixture in step 3. Substitute mushroom strips for pork in step 4, leaving them in pan when cooked. Continue with master recipe, substituting 4 cups shredded bok choy (greens only—see figures 14 and 16, pages 68–69) for napa cabbage.

COLD SESAME NOODLES

Cold sesame noodles, a popular item on Chinese restaurant menus, are easy to make at home. The noodles are simply boiled, oiled, chilled, and then tossed with a smooth dressing.

As we found with lo mein, traditional recipes call for fresh Chinese egg noodles, but we wanted to see if other noodles could be successfully substituted. Chinese sesame paste is a traditional component of the sauce. Since it is available only in Asian food stores, we wondered how tahini (a Middle Eastern sesame paste sold in most supermarkets) or peanut butter would perform.

As we expected, fresh Chinese egg noodles performed best in this dish, cooking up tender but not mushy. In fact, we soon realized that this soft texture is a major difference between Chinese and Western pasta dishes, where a springier, chewier texture is prized. Frozen Chinese egg noodles, which require an extra two minutes of cooking time, worked well, too.

We wondered if fresh Italian pasta, which served as a good substitute for fresh Chinese noodles in lo mein, would also do the job here. Our tests initially looked promising, but the noodles continued to absorb sauce as they sat, eventually became very mushy. In fact, noodles that were pretty good at the outset collapsed under the weight of the sauce after just 10 minutes.

This time dried Italian pasta—spaghetti—eventually proved to be the best substitute. When cooked until al dente, the pasta did not absorb the sauce as well as fresh egg noodles and its texture was too springy. Somewhat surprisingly, when we overcooked dried Italian spaghetti (it was cooked a full 15 minutes), we had much better results. Now the pasta was soft, just like fresh Chinese egg noodles. Because dried spaghetti swells much more than fresh pasta, we found we needed a smaller amount of spaghetti than Chinese noodles to achieve the same volume of cooked noodles.

Our success with dried Chinese noodles varied by brand. When cooked till soft, the noodles in some brands became mushy or even fell apart when sauced. We eventually found some brands that held their shape better, but since all brands of dried spaghetti worked fine, we recommend that you stick with Italian pasta as a substitute for fresh Chinese egg noodles in this dish.

In our testing of the sauce, we substituted both tahini and peanut butter for Chinese sesame paste and found that peanut butter contributed a nuttier flavor that comes closer to that of Chinese sesame paste. Surprisingly, tasters reported that the sauce made with peanut butter tasted "nutty" but did not detect a "peanuty" flavor. Tahini has a nice creamy texture, but the nut flavor is rather muted. Choose a smooth peanut butter made without sugar (look for a natural brand) for the best results.

A wide array of seasonings were called for in the sesame noodle recipes we looked at, including ginger, garlic, sake, coriander, hoisin sauce, soy sauce, honey, Szechuan pepper, and balsamic vinegar. Ginger and garlic were the most common, but we found their flavors too harsh when raw. Other seasonings, such as hoisin sauce and Szechuan pepper, competed with the nut flavor. In the end, we chose very simple seasonings to round out the flavors: soy sauce to add a salty note, some rice vinegar for acidity, a little hot sauce for heat, and some sugar to keep everything in balance.

Water is used to thin the sauce, and hot is preferable to cold for its ability to release more flavor. We found it best to let the sauce rest at room temperature for 30 minutes to allow flavors to develop and to ensure that the sugar dissolves.

We found that mixing the pasta with the sauce and then refrigerating for any amount of time results in a rather dry and sticky mixture, no matter how much oil and water the sauce contains. It is best to mix the sauce with the chilled and oiled pasta just before serving to ensure the creamiest result.

Master Recipe

Cold Sesame Noodles

serves 4 to 6

➤ NOTE: *Smooth peanut butter (use a natural brand without added sugar) is a better substitute for difficult-to-find Chinese sesame paste than the somewhat bland Middle Eastern–style tahini. But if you can find real Chinese sesame paste, by all means use it. We like some heat in the sauce (it helps to cut the richness), but you can omit the hot sauce if you prefer. Toasting the sesame seeds in a dry skillet until they achieve a rich golden color will boost their flavor.*

1	tablespoon salt
1	pound fresh Chinese egg noodles (the width of spaghetti) or ¾ pound dried Italian spaghetti
2	tablespoons Asian sesame oil
½	cup smooth natural peanut butter
3	tablespoons soy sauce
1	tablespoon sugar
1	tablespoon rice vinegar
½	teaspoon hot sauce, such as chili paste or Tabasco, or more to taste
½	cup hot water, or more
4	scallions, white and light green parts, finely chopped
2	tablespoons sesame seeds, toasted

INSTRUCTIONS:

1. Bring 6 quarts water to a boil in large pot. Add salt and noodles and cook until noodles are just tender, 3 to 4 minutes. (If using dried Italian spaghetti, cook noodles until quite soft, about 15 minutes.) Drain thoroughly and toss with oil. Cool to room temperature. Cover and refrigerate until ready to use, at least 2 hours and up to 1 day.

2. Place peanut butter, soy sauce, sugar, vinegar, and hot sauce in blender or food processor. Process until smooth. With motor running, add water, 1 tablespoon at a time, until sauce is the consistency of heavy cream. Scrape sauce into large bowl and set aside for 30 minutes to allow flavors to blend. (Can be covered and set aside for several hours. Stir in hot water, a tablespoon at a time, if sauce thickens.)

3. When ready to serve, separate noodles with your fingers and then toss them with peanut sauce and scallions. Sprinkle with sesame seeds and serve immediately.

Cold Sesame Noodles with Chicken and Vegetables
serves 4 as a main course

➤ **NOTE:** *The addition of chicken and fresh vegetables makes this a good main dish choice in warm weather. It is assembled in the fashion of a composed salad, with the vegetables and roasted chicken arranged on top of the noodles.*

Salt

1 pound fresh Chinese egg noodles (the width of spaghetti) or ¾ pound dried Italian spaghetti

2 tablespoons Asian sesame oil

1 whole chicken breast (bone in, skin on), about ¾ pound

1 tablespoon vegetable oil

¾ cup smooth natural peanut butter

4½ tablespoons soy sauce

1½ tablespoons sugar

1½ tablespoons rice vinegar

¾ teaspoon hot sauce, such as chili paste or Tabasco, or more to taste

¾ cup hot water, or more

2 medium cucumbers

½ medium carrot, peeled

(Ingredients continued on next page)

(Ingredients continued from previous page)

½	**medium red bell pepper, cored, seeded, and cut into thin strips**
4	**scallions, white and light green parts, finely chopped**
2	**tablespoons sesame seeds, toasted**

⁝⁝ I N S T R U C T I O N S :

1. Bring 6 quarts water to a boil in large pot. Add 1 tablespoon salt and noodles and cook until noodles are just tender, 3 to 4 minutes. (If using dried Italian spaghetti, cook noodles until quite soft, about 15 minutes.) Drain thoroughly and toss with sesame oil. Cool to room temperature. Cover and refrigerate until ready to use, at least 2 hours and up to 1 day.

2. Meanwhile, preheat oven to 400 degrees. Rub chicken with vegetable oil and sprinkle generously with salt and place in roasting pan. Roast until meat thermometer inserted into thickest part of breast registers 160 degrees, 35 to 40 minutes. Cool to room temperature, remove skin, and shred meat into bite-sized pieces.

3. Place peanut butter, soy sauce, sugar, vinegar, and hot sauce in blender or food processor. Process until smooth. With motor running, add water, 1 tablespoon at a time, until sauce is the consistency of heavy cream. Scrape sauce into large bowl and set aside for 30 minutes to allow flavors to blend. (Can be covered and set aside for several hours. Stir in hot water, a tablespoon at a time, if sauce thickens.)

4. Peel cucumbers and halve lengthwise. Use spoon to scoop out and discard seeds. Using large holes of a box grater, grate cucumbers and then squeeze dry in clean kitchen towel. Grate carrot, and prepare bell pepper.

5. When ready to serve, separate noodles with your fingers and then toss them with 1¼ cups peanut sauce and scallions. Arrange noodles on large platter or individual plates. Toss cucumber, carrot, and bell pepper together and arrange on top of noodles. Pile chicken in center. Drizzle remaining sauce over chicken and vegetables and sprinkle with sesame seeds. Serve immediately.

index